Bible Tell Me WHO

Lessons from Amazing People of the Bible

Christopher D. Hudson

Illustrated by Pascale Lafond

Time
HOME ENTERTAINMENT

TIME HOME ENTERTAINMENT

PUBLISHER
Jim Childs

VICE PRESIDENT, BRAND & DIGITAL STRATEGY
Steven Sandonato

EXECUTIVE DIRECTOR, MARKETING SERVICES
Carol Pittard

EXECUTIVE DIRECTOR, RETAIL & SPECIAL SALES
Tom Mifsud

EXECUTIVE PUBLISHING DIRECTOR
Joy Butts

DIRECTOR, BOOKAZINE DEVELOPMENT & MARKETING
Laura Adam

FINANCE DIRECTOR
Glenn Buonocore

ASSOCIATE PUBLISHING DIRECTOR
Megan Pearlman

ASSOCIATE GENERAL COUNSEL
Helen Wan

ASSISTANT DIRECTOR, SPECIAL SALES
Ilene Schreider

BRAND MANAGER, PRODUCT MARKETING
Nina Fleishman Reed

ASSOCIATE PRODUCTION MANAGER
Kimberly Marshall

ASSOCIATE PREPRESS MANAGER
Alex Voznesenskiy

EDITORIAL DIRECTOR
Stephen Koepp

COPY CHIEF
Rina Bander

DESIGN MANAGER
Anne-Michelle Gallero

SPECIAL THANKS: Katherine Barnet, Jeremy Biloon,
Dana Campolattaro, Susan Chodakiewicz, Rose Cirrincione,
Assu Etsubneh, Jacqueline Fitzgerald, Christine Font,
Hillary Hirsch, David Kahn, Amy Mangus, Nina Mistry,
Dave Rozzelle, Ricardo Santiago, Gina Scauzillo,
Adriana Tierno, Vanessa Wu

DESIGN AND PRODUCTION
Mark Wainwright, Symbology Creative

ILLUSTRATION
Pascale Lafond
Illustrations used with permission of TheBiblePeople.com

CONTENT AND DEVELOPMENT
Christopher D. Hudson
HudsonBible.com

EDITORIAL ACKNOWLEDGEMENTS
Ben Irwin, Brooke Keith, Mary Larsen, Stephen Leston, Robin Merrill, Melissa Peitsch,
and Jennifer Turner

© 2013 **Time Home Entertainment Inc.**
Published by Time Home Entertainment Inc.
135 West 50th Street • New York, NY 10020

ISBN 10: **1-61893-098-2**
ISBN 13: **978-1-61893-098-9**
Library of Congress Control Number: **2013947385**

We welcome your comments and suggestions about Time Home Entertainment Books.
Please write to us at:
Time Home Entertainment Books
Attention: Book Editors
PO Box 11016
Des Moines, IA 50336-1016

If you would like to order any of our hardcover Collector's Edition books,
please call us at 1-800-327-6388, Monday through Friday, 7 a.m. to 8 p.m.,
or Saturday, 7 a.m. to 6 p.m., Central Time.

Introduction

Welcome to a great adventure! In these pages, you will meet some great heroes and some awful villains of the Bible. Pay close attention as you read, because you will learn from all of them! When you learn about these people, you will find out how much God loves you. You will also discover how you should live and how you can love God.

Table of Contents

Lessons from Amazing People of the Bible

Adam and Eve
The First Man and Woman

God made Adam and Eve. He placed them in a garden where they had everything they needed. The only thing they could not have was the fruit from a special tree. God told them to leave this fruit alone. Satan, God's enemy, had a plan to trick them. He made himself look like a snake. He told Eve that if she ate the fruit, she would be like God. Eve disobeyed God and ate the fruit. Then she told Adam, and he ate it too. Right away, they both knew they had done something very wrong.

What can we learn from Adam and Eve?

Just like Adam and Eve, we were also made by God. Because God made us, he knows what is best for us. If we listen to God and obey him, our lives will be easier. Disobeying God always brings trouble.

9

Satan
The Enemy of God

Before God made people, God made the angels. They worshiped God and worked for him. Satan was one of the angels, but he wanted to be God and rule the world his way. Because Satan didn't obey God, God sent him away from heaven. Satan talked Adam and Eve into disobeying God. Since then, Satan has tried to get people to turn away from God. But he will never be more powerful than God.

What can we learn from Satan's sin?

We can never be bigger or better than God! He's the only One who has the power and love it takes to rule the world and our hearts.

Cain and Abel
The Sons of Adam and Eve

God still loved Adam and Eve and gave them children. Their first two sons were named Cain and Abel. When Cain grew up, he became a farmer. When Abel grew up, he became a shepherd. One day, they brought gifts to God from their crops and animals. God was pleased with Abel's offering because it was his best. God was not pleased with Cain's gift. Cain felt jealous of Abel, so he killed his brother.

What can we learn from Cain and Abel?

Cain made some awful decisions because he was jealous and selfish. By choosing to be selfish instead of loving God, Cain made bad choices. He hurt himself and everyone around him.

Noah
The Man Who Built the Ark

During Noah's time, people behaved very badly. They thought only of themselves and did not love God. They behaved so badly that God thought the best thing to do was to start all over. He sent a flood to destroy all the evil on earth. But because Noah and his family loved God, God saved them. He warned them of the flood, and he told Noah to build a big boat called an ark.

What can we learn from Noah?

While Noah was working so hard to build the ark, other people may have stood around making fun of him. Noah stayed strong. He did what God told him to do. God's words are always true. We can trust what he says no matter how strange it seems to others.

Job

The Man Who Loved God No Matter What

Job was a faithful man who loved God very much. Satan thought Job would stop loving God if his life was full of pain and suffering. God allowed Satan to make Job suffer, but God told Satan not to let Job die. Satan got busy. In one day, all of Job's animals were either stolen or killed. All of his servants were also killed. Then all ten of his children died. Then Job's body broke out in painful sores! Job was sad and in pain, but he never stopped loving God. Later, God blessed Job with ten more children and more animals than he had before.

What can we learn from Job?

Bad things happen in life sometimes. When they do happen, we have two choices. We can get angry and choose to stop loving God or we can trust God anyway. We can praise God and thank him for loving us no matter what happens to us!

Abraham

The Father of Many Nations

Abraham was a good man who loved God, and God loved him. God called him his friend! One day, God told Abraham to leave his home. Abraham obeyed. He and his wife, Sarah, packed up everything they owned. They walked until they came to a new land. Abraham did not have any children yet. But God promised him that he would one day be the father of many people. This new land would be their home!

What can we learn from Abraham?

God always knows what is best for us. We can trust him when he tells us to do something. God always keeps his promises. Because God is honest with us, we can obey and follow him.

20

Sarah
The Wife of Abraham

In the days of the Old Testament, people lived to be very old. When Sarah was 90 years old and her husband Abraham was 100, God told them they would have a baby. Sarah laughed. She was too old to have a baby! But God is faithful. There is nothing too hard for him. Sarah gave birth to a son, and they named him Isaac. When he grew up, he loved and served God.

What can we learn from Sarah?

Even when something seems too hard for God, he can do it. His promises are real and true. When God says he will do something, he will!

Lot
The Man Who Escaped

Almost everyone who lived in the cities of Sodom and Gomorrah turned away from God. Lot was the only person who obeyed God. When God decided to destroy the cities, he sent two angels to save Lot. The angels helped Lot and his family run away as fast as they could. The angels warned Lot's family not to look back. But Lot's wife didn't listen. She looked back and turned into a block of salt!

What can we learn from Lot?

Lot chose to follow God even when no one else did. It's not always easy to make the right choices and do good things. But God helps us do what is right!

23

Hagar

The Servant Who Was Sent Away

God promised Abraham many children. But Abraham's wife, Sarah, had not been able to have a baby yet. Sarah asked Abraham to have a baby with Hagar. Hagar had a baby named Ishmael. This made Abraham happy. Sarah became jealous. She began to dislike Hagar and Ishmael. Later, Sarah had her own child, Isaac. She didn't want Isaac to have to share with Ishmael. Sarah asked Abraham to send Hagar and Ishmael away.

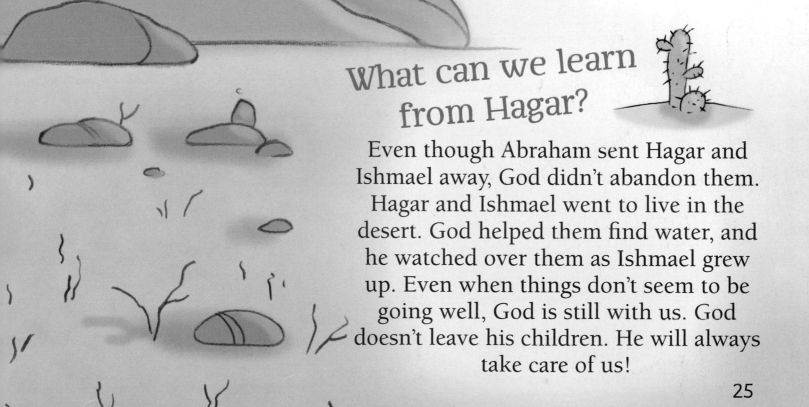

What can we learn from Hagar?

Even though Abraham sent Hagar and Ishmael away, God didn't abandon them. Hagar and Ishmael went to live in the desert. God helped them find water, and he watched over them as Ishmael grew up. Even when things don't seem to be going well, God is still with us. God doesn't leave his children. He will always take care of us!

Ishmael
The Big Brother

Ishmael and Isaac were half brothers. They lived close to each other for a few years before Ishmael moved away with his mother, Hagar. Ishmael was older than Isaac. He was the big brother. One day Isaac's mother, Sarah, saw Ishmael making fun of Isaac. He wasn't being a nice brother. This made Sarah very angry.

What can we learn from Ishmael?

Sometimes family members don't get along with each other. But even when things aren't perfect, God still wants us to be kind to our brothers and sisters. Ishmael should have been kind to Isaac. No matter what happens, we can respond with kindness, even when our brothers and sisters are trying to annoy us!

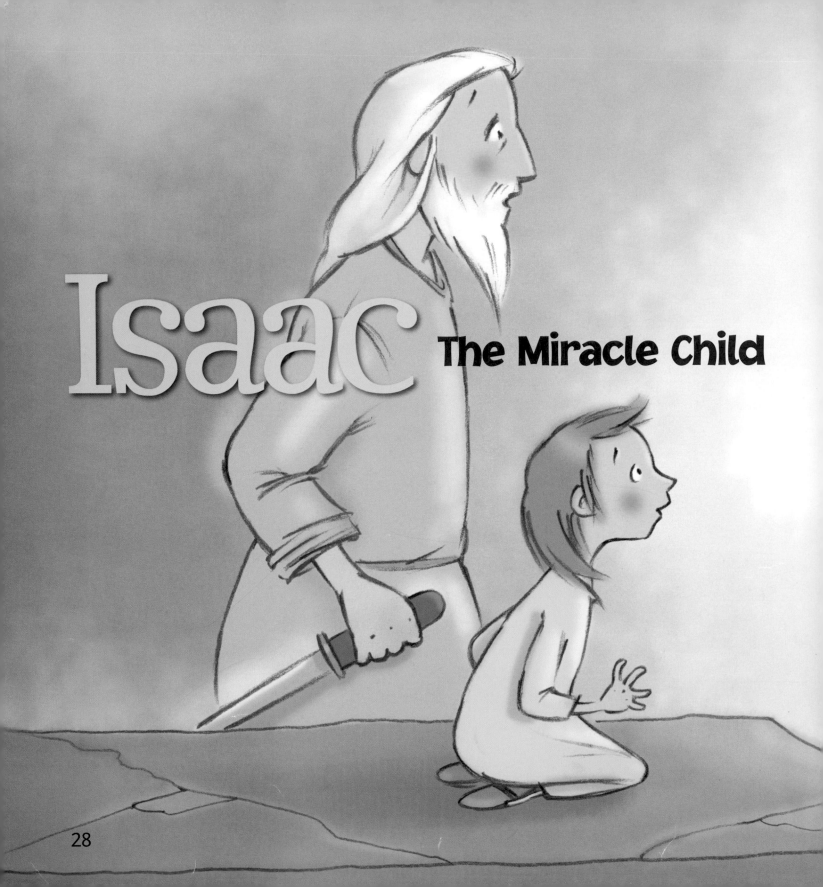

Isaac
The Miracle Child

Isaac's parents were very old when he was born. They loved their son, but God wanted to know if they loved God more. God tested Abraham by asking him to sacrifice, or kill, his son. In those days, people would show love for God by sacrificing animals. Abraham obeyed God and took Isaac to a mountain. Abraham was ready to kill his own son, but God saved Isaac and sent a ram for Abraham to sacrifice instead.

What can we learn from Isaac?

God saved Isaac, and Isaac trusted and loved God. God saves us too. We can always rest in his love.

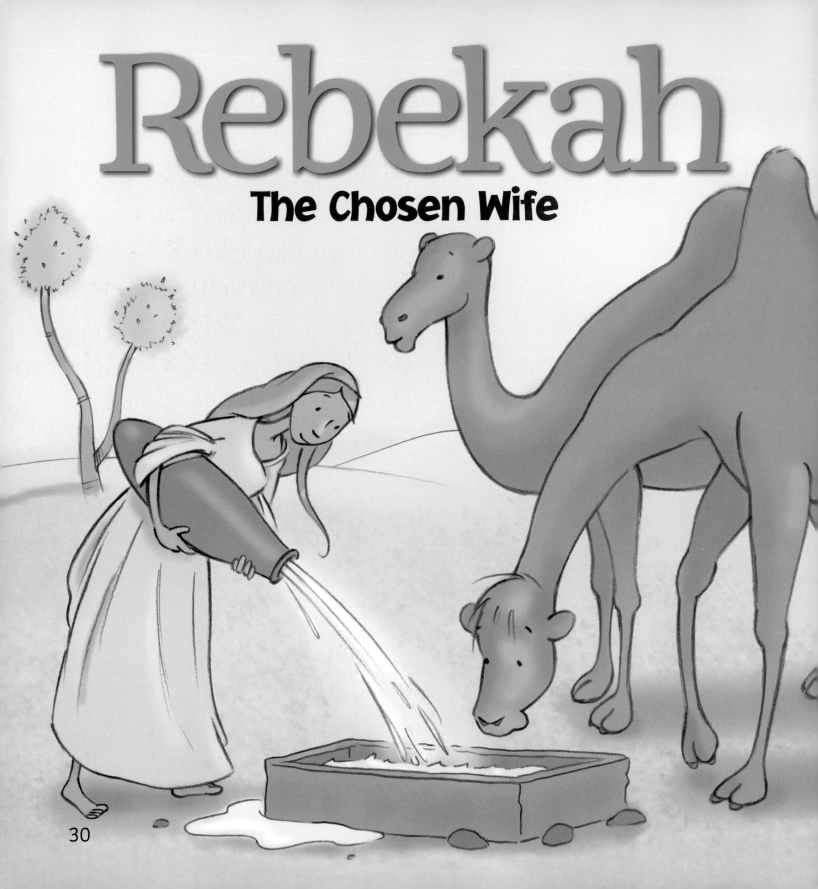

Rebekah

The Chosen Wife

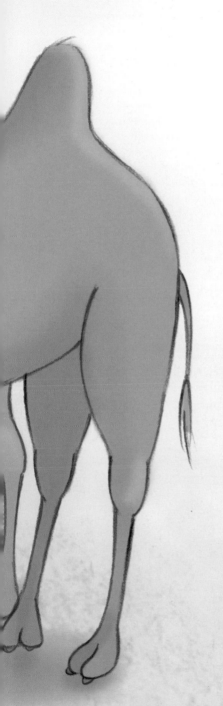

When Isaac grew up, Abraham sent his trusted servant to another country to find the right wife for his son. When the servant got there, he stopped at a well. He prayed and asked God to let the right woman give him and his camels a drink. Before he finished praying, the servant saw Rebekah walking toward the well! She was the right wife for Isaac. Rebekah agreed to return with Abraham's servant and marry Isaac.

What can we learn from Rebekah?

Most people wouldn't want to marry a total stranger! But Rebekah left her family and moved to a new land. She believed God had chosen her to marry Isaac. We can trust God and believe that his plans are always the best for us.

31

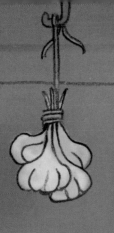

God gave Isaac and Rebekah twin boys named Jacob and Esau. Esau was born first. As he grew up, he spent his time hunting outside. Jacob enjoyed cooking and staying at home. One day, Esau came home feeling very hungry, and he asked his brother for a meal. Jacob gave Esau a bowl of stew, but he made Esau pay for it. Jacob asked Esau for his birthrights. A birthright was a special reward for being the oldest son. Esau traded a single meal for his birthrights.

What can we learn from Esau?

Esau didn't think about what would happen after he ate his stew. He just wanted to eat. God wants us to think before we act so we can make wise choices.

Jacob
The Blessing Stealer

God had a special plan for Jacob. But Jacob didn't always trust God or do what he knew was right. One day, Jacob pretended to be his twin brother so he could trick his father, Isaac. While Esau was out hunting, Jacob put on Esau's clothes. Because Isaac was almost blind, Isaac thought Jacob was Esau. He gave his blessing to Jacob instead of to Esau. This meant Jacob would receive all the family honors that should have been given to Esau. Jacob stole from his brother!

What can we learn from Jacob?

Jacob should have been truthful to his father and kind to his brother. God loves when we tell the truth and treat people with kindness.

Leah and Rachel
The Sisters Who Shared a Husband

Jacob took one look at Rachel and fell in love. He asked her dad, Laban, if he could marry her if he worked for Laban for seven years. Laban said, "Of course!" After the seven years passed, it was time for the wedding day. But Laban lied! He gave Leah, Rachel's older sister, to Jacob instead of Rachel. Jacob was really mad! Leah was a good woman, but Jacob did not love her. He loved Rachel. Laban said Jacob could marry Rachel if he worked for him for another seven years. So Jacob married Rachel too. The sisters didn't get along with each other because they had to share Jacob as their husband.

What can we learn from Leah and Rachel?

Life was hard for Leah and Rachel, but God still protected them. No matter how hard things get in our families, God will always protect us.

Levi and Simeon

The Brothers Who Took Revenge

Levi and Simeon were two of Joseph's brothers. Dinah was their sister. A man named Shechem hurt Dinah badly. Her brothers were very angry. They came up with a plan to get back at Shechem.

Levi and Simeon snuck up on the men in Shechem's town and killed them all. They took away everything they had—their animals, their wives, and their children. But Jacob (Levi and Simeon's father) was very upset with his sons. What they had done was very wrong!

What can we learn from Levi and Simeon?

Shechem was guilty of a crime, but it was wrong for Levi and Simeon to take revenge. God says he will pay back people who do bad things. Instead of doing bad things to people who hurt us, we should trust God to make things right.

40

Judah

The Man Who Sold His Brother into Slavery

Joseph's brothers didn't like him. They were mean to him and talked about killing him. They even stuck him in a hole. But Joseph's brother Judah spoke up. He told his brothers not to kill Joseph. Instead, the brothers sold Joseph as a slave. Then they told their poor father that Joseph had died.

What can we learn from Judah?

Joseph's brothers wanted to kill him, but his brother Judah saved his life. God had an amazing plan for Joseph, and he has a plan for us too. God can turn bad things into good things!

41

Potiphar

The Man Who Put Joseph in Prison

After Joseph had been taken to Egypt, he was sold as a slave to a man named Potiphar. Joseph worked hard. Potiphar trusted him and put him in charge of everything in his house. There was just one problem: Potiphar's wife. She liked Joseph and thought he was handsome. But Joseph stayed away from her. That made her mad! She lied to her husband about Joseph and told him Joseph had treated her badly. Potiphar believed his wife, so he sent Joseph to prison.

What can we learn from Potiphar?

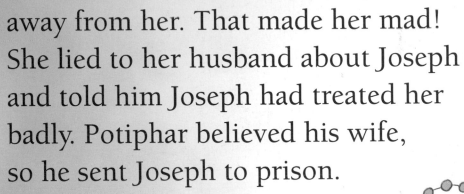

Joseph had been such a good worker in Potiphar's house. But Potiphar was quick to believe the bad things he heard about Joseph. Not all bad things we hear are true. We should never believe everything we hear about our friends or say mean things about them. That's gossip, and it can really hurt people's feelings.

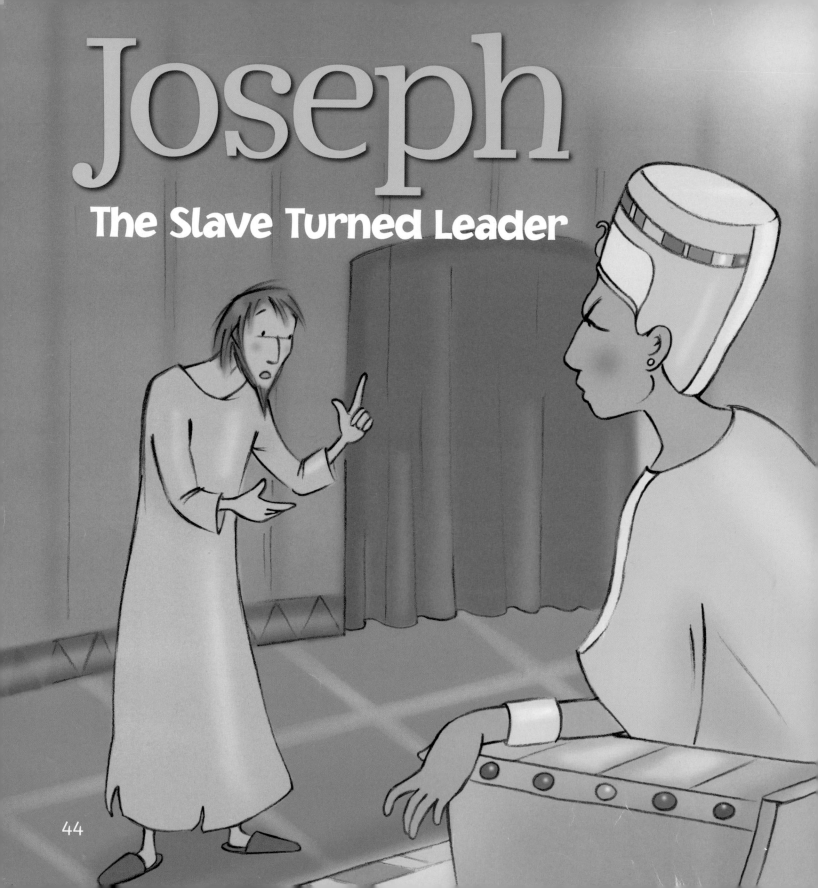

Joseph

The Slave Turned Leader

Joseph worked as a slave in the land of Egypt. Then he was sent to prison for something he didn't do. While he was in prison, he told people the secret meanings of their dreams. Everything he said came true! Pharaoh, the king of Egypt, asked Joseph to tell him the meaning of his dream too. Joseph told him, and Pharaoh was so happy that he let Joseph rule over all the land. Joseph ended up saving many people from hunger because he was put in charge of the food in the land.

What can we learn from Joseph?

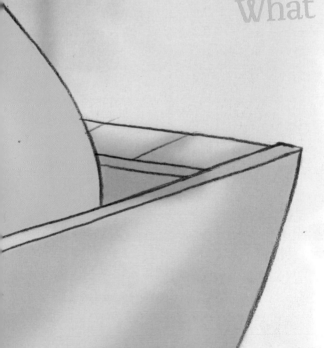

Joseph had been stuck in jail. But God did not let him down. God used Joseph's time in jail to prepare him to lead a whole country and save people's lives. God will never, ever let us down. God was faithful to Joseph in his troubles. He will be faithful to us too!

Benjamin

The Youngest Brother

46

Benjamin was a baby when his older brothers sold Joseph into slavery. Years later, Benjamin's brothers traveled to Egypt to buy food. Joseph was in charge of the food, but his brothers didn't know who Joseph was. Joseph asked them to bring their youngest brother, Benjamin, to Egypt. When they did, Joseph gave them a feast and fed Benjamin the most food. When Joseph saw that his brothers truly loved Benjamin, he knew their hearts had changed. He told them who he was—their long-lost brother Joseph! He loved them and forgave them.

What can we learn from Benjamin?

Joseph loved his brother Benjamin and was very kind to him. He was also kind to his other brothers, even though they had been mean to him. God loves us even when we make bad choices and do bad things. He loves us no matter what we do.

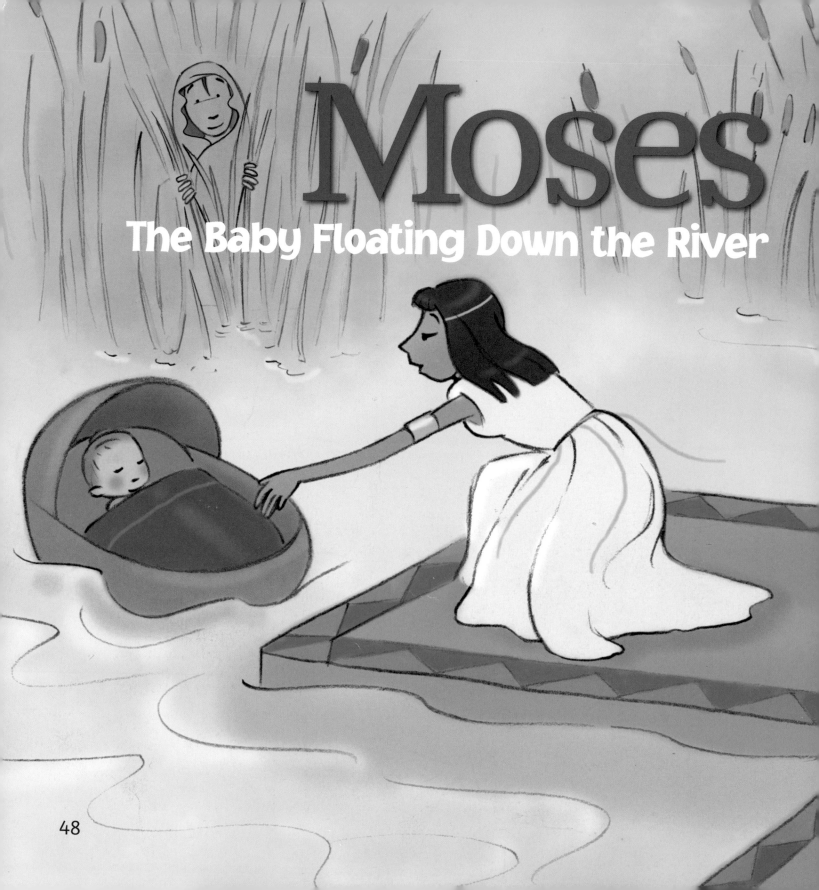

Moses

The Baby Floating Down the River

Pharaoh was a bad, bad king. He had ordered all Hebrew baby boys killed! Can you imagine how scary this was for Moses' mother? She had to do something to save her baby boy. So she put him in a basket and sent him safely floating down the river. Pharaoh's daughter found him. She raised him as her son. Moses' real mom was able to care for him when he was little. Moses would grow up to save his people.

What can we learn from Moses?

Moses went from floating down a river to becoming a great leader of God's people! God worked it all out in an amazing way. When things get scary, we can trust in God. He always has a plan.

49

Aaron
The Speaker and Priest

Aaron was Moses' brother. Moses sometimes had trouble talking, but Aaron was a good speaker. So Aaron would often speak for Moses. He would stand before the Hebrew people and tell them the messages that God had given to Moses. Aaron also went with Moses to tell Pharaoh God's messages. Pharaoh used the Hebrew people as slaves, and God wanted Pharaoh to let his people go free. Aaron obeyed God, and God chose him to be a high priest. A high priest had the special job of talking to God for the people. He also stood before God to offer sacrifices for the sins of the people.

What can we learn from Aaron?

As the high priest, Aaron helped people talk with God. But we do not need anyone to help us talk to God. Jesus came to be our high priest. Because Jesus died and was willing to be punished in our place for our sins, we can talk to God anytime we want!

51

Pharaoh

The Stubborn King

Pharaoh kept God's people in slavery. God sent Moses and Aaron to tell Pharaoh to set his people free. Pharaoh wouldn't listen, even after God sent plagues of frogs, gnats, flies, painful sores, hailstones, locusts, and darkness. After every plague, Pharaoh said he would let God's people go. Then he would change his mind. Finally, after his oldest son died, Pharaoh let Moses and the people go. But then Pharaoh changed his mind again. He and his army chased God's people. God parted the Red Sea so his people could safely cross. Pharaoh's army drowned in the water.

What can we learn from Pharaoh?

Pharaoh just would not listen to Moses and Aaron! He was stubborn and refused to hear God's messages to him. When God speaks, we need to listen!

Joshua

The Man Who Trusted God

Canaan was the land that God had promised to God's people. Before God's people entered Canaan, Moses sent twelve men to explore the land. Joshua was one of those men. The men came back and reported that big, tall, scary-looking people lived in Canaan. So God's people were worried they might be killed if they entered the land! But Joshua and another man, Caleb, trusted God. They said, "The land is good! We should enter Canaan because God is with us." The people who didn't trust God got sick and died, but Joshua and Caleb lived.

Later, God chose Joshua to lead the people into the promised land.

What can we learn from Joshua?

Joshua trusted God and knew that God would take care of his people. He wasn't afraid to obey God and live in the promised land. Sometimes there are scary things in life and we forget to trust God to help us. But God watches over us, and we can always trust him.

Rahab

The Sinful Woman Who Was Saved

Rahab was a sinful woman who lived in Jericho, a city in the promised land of Canaan. Rahab hid two Israelite spies in her house. She kept them safe from men who were looking for them in Jericho. She told the Israelite spies that she believed in God. She knew the land of Canaan belonged to God's people. The spies promised to keep her and her family safe when the Israelites destroyed Jericho. Rahab hung a red rope outside her house so they would remember their promise to her. When the time came for the Israelites to destroy Jericho, Rahab and her family were saved.

What can we learn from Rahab?

Rahab was a sinful person, but God cared about her. He saved her because she trusted in him. God is a God of mercy. He will forgive us when we trust in him. The red rope on Rahab's house was like the blood of Jesus. His blood covers our sins and saves us!

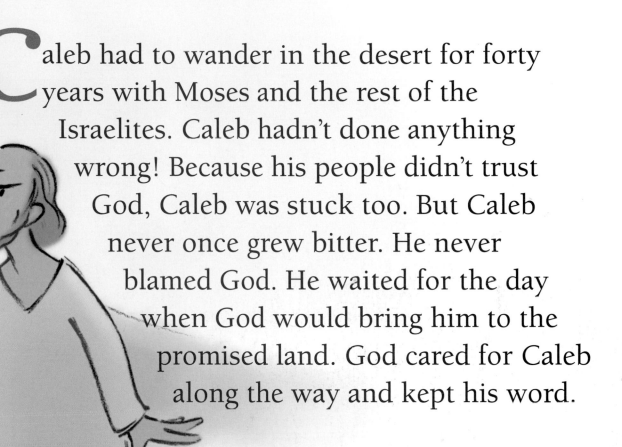

Caleb had to wander in the desert for forty years with Moses and the rest of the Israelites. Caleb hadn't done anything wrong! Because his people didn't trust God, Caleb was stuck too. But Caleb never once grew bitter. He never blamed God. He waited for the day when God would bring him to the promised land. God cared for Caleb along the way and kept his word.

What can we learn from Caleb?

Sometimes people do things that hurt us and make our lives harder. Like Caleb, we can trust God. We can be brave and remember that God stays with us until the end!

Deborah

The Brave Judge

After Joshua died, the people of Israel forgot how good God had been to them. They disobeyed God. God gave them judges to lead them. Deborah was one of those judges. She trusted God. While she was a judge, a mean king and the cruel leader of his army had taken charge over the Israelites. To save God's people, Deborah told a soldier named Barak to fight the enemy king and his army. She promised that God would help the Israelites win the battle. The leader of the army, Sisera, ran and hid in the tent that belonged to his friend's wife. The friend's wife killed him. God's people won!

What can we learn from Deborah?

Deborah was faithful to God even in a time of evil. She obeyed God and helped her people beat their enemies. There is a lot of evil in our world. But there is also a lot of good if we are willing to share it.

Gideon
The Mighty Warrior

God's people forgot to listen to him again. They hid from their neighbors, the Midianites. An angel came to a man named Gideon. The angel said, "God is with you. Be strong and fight. Save God's people!" But Gideon did not feel strong. He gathered 32,000 men to fight with him. God told him to take only 300 men. Gideon and his men went to the Midianite camp at night. They blew trumpets, broke jars, and waved torches. When the Midianites woke up confused, they fought each other!

What can we learn from Gideon?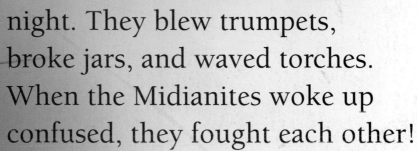

Gideon found out that God can do anything! God may ask you to do something that seems hard. Maybe he wants you to tell someone about him or give away a toy. It might seem hard to do, but God will always make a way for you to do what he asks!

Samson

The Muscle Man

amson was the leader of Israel. He was amazingly strong, and he fought Israel's enemies, the Philistines. Samson fell in love with Delilah, a beautiful Philistine woman. The Philistine leaders asked her to trick Samson in order to find out why he was so strong. Samson told her, "It's my long hair!" As he took a nap, she cut off his hair. His strength was gone! The Philistines grabbed him and made him blind. Then they threw him in jail. But while he was in jail, Samson's hair started to grow back. God made him strong again. One night, the Philistines had a big party. They brought out Samson to make fun of him. He stood between two posts in the building, and he pushed against them with all his might. The roof of the building crashed down on his enemies.

What can we learn from Samson?

Samson's strength didn't really come from his long hair. It came from God. Samson's long hair was just a sign that God was with Samson. We can trust God to give us strength to help us through hard times.

Ruth
The Loyal Daughter-in-Law

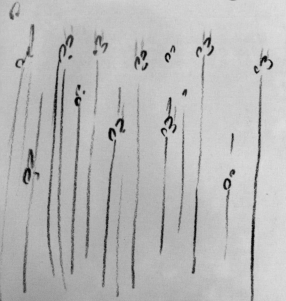

Naomi was an old woman. Her husband and two sons had died. Ruth was a young woman who had been married to one of Naomi's sons. Naomi wanted to move back to her home in Bethlehem. She told Ruth to stay and find a new husband. But Ruth said, "I will go where you go." Ruth could not stand to be away from Naomi. So she went with her and took care of her. While looking for food in the fields so Naomi would not go hungry, Ruth met her future husband. God took care of Ruth and blessed her family. In fact, her great-grandson was King David!

What can we learn from Ruth?

Because Ruth loved Naomi in her time of need, more love came back to her. We should always care for others as Ruth did. When we do, we show the world how much God loves us!

Samuel
The Boy Who Listened to God

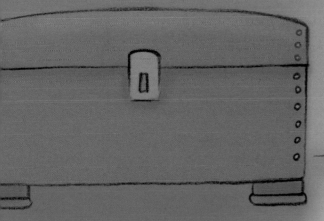

amuel was a young boy who worked in the temple with Eli the priest. One night while Samuel was sleeping, he heard someone call, "Samuel!" Samuel answered, "Yes, Eli?" But Eli was not calling him. Two more times Samuel heard the voice, but it wasn't Eli. Eli told him to answer next time because it could be God's voice. When the voice called again, Samuel said, "I'm listening. What do you want me to do?" God gave Samuel a message to tell others. He told Samuel what he was about to do. Samuel became a prophet and followed God for the rest of his life.

What can we learn from Samuel?

Eli was God's priest, but God chose to speak to a young boy named Samuel. God has created all of us for a purpose. No matter how big or small we are, we all have a purpose in this world!

The Philistines

The Enemy of the Israelites

The Philistines and the Israelites didn't like each other. They often fought. One day, the Philistines took the special chest of God from the Israelites. The chest was a symbol of God's presence with his people. It held the Ten Commandments that God had given his people long ago. The Philistines didn't love or honor God. God caused a lot of trouble for them because they took his special chest. Horrible sores covered their bodies, and many of them died! The Philistines quickly gave the sacred chest back to God's people!

What can we learn from the Philistines?

The Philistines did not love or respect God. They did not deserve to be near God. Because Jesus died for us, we can be close to him. Like the children of Israel, we are God's people too.

King Saul

The Good King
Gone Wrong

King Saul was chosen as the first king of Israel. At first he was a good king, but then he started making bad choices. One time, the Philistines were ready to attack. Their army was much bigger than Israel's army. Saul was worried. He knew he needed God's help to win, but he didn't ask God for help in the right way. He broke one of God's laws because he didn't wait for the prophet Samuel to come and offer a sacrifice to God. Later, Saul refused to let the men in his army eat for a whole day. Another time, Saul ordered one of his men to kill all the people in a place called Nob—even women and children! Saul kept making awful choices.

What can we learn from King Saul?

Saul should have made better choices by listening to Samuel and obeying God. We can make bad choices too. Instead of getting deeper into sin, we should stop and listen to God. His ideas are always best.

David

The Boy Who Killed a Giant

David was just a small boy. Goliath was a big, mean Philistine. The Israelite soldiers were afraid of him. No one felt brave enough to fight a giant. But David wasn't afraid. He said he would fight Goliath. The soldiers thought David was too young, but David didn't think so. With a small rock from his slingshot and help from God, David killed Goliath.

What can we learn from David?

David wasn't afraid of Goliath. David knew he was small. He also knew Goliath was big. But David knew one thing that no one else could understand—God was bigger. With God's help, anything is possible!

Goliath
The Giant Guy Who Opened His Big Mouth

Goliath was a Philistine giant who was over nine feet tall! He was super mean to the Israelites. He was so big, strong, and tall that none of the Israelites would fight him. They all ran away and hid! Goliath opened his big mouth and said, "Your God must not be so strong if all your soldiers are afraid of me." David said, "I will fight you!" And with one small rock from his sling, David killed Goliath!

What can we learn from Goliath?

Goliath made a big mistake. He thought he was so big and strong that nothing could stop him. Boy, was he wrong! Our God is such a big God. There isn't anyone, anything, or any problem too big for him! God helps little people do big things!

Jonathan

The Best Friend Ever

When David was young, he would play his harp for King Saul. His music made Saul feel better when he was upset. But soon, Saul became jealous of David because God had chosen him to be the next king of Israel. Saul even threw a spear at David and tried to kill him! Saul's son Jonathan was David's best friend. He didn't like how his dad treated David. Jonathan helped David escape from King Saul. Jonathan and David promised to be friends forever.

What can we learn from Jonathan?

Jonathan was the king's son. Yet he wasn't jealous of David, who would be the next king instead of him. Unlike Saul, Jonathan chose to be kind to David. We can choose to do what is right too. We can set a good example for grown-ups.

Solomon
The Wisest Man Ever

After King David became very old, he died. He left his kingdom to his son Solomon. One night, God came to Solomon in a dream. God said that Solomon could ask for anything he wanted, and he would receive it. Wow! Can you imagine God asking you, "What can I do for you?" Solomon could have asked for gold or silver. He could have asked for power and fame. He could have asked for anything! But Solomon asked for wisdom, and he received it. God was very happy with what Solomon asked for. Solomon was the wisest man ever because his wisdom came from God.

What can we learn from Solomon?

God gave Solomon wisdom, but Solomon was already pretty smart because he knew what to ask God for. He knew that he could not be a good king without God's help. He needed the wisdom of God to lead his people. We should always seek God's wisdom for our lives too.

81

Josiah

The Boy King

Josiah was a special kid. He was also a king. Imagine becoming king at only eight years old! *Wow!* Josiah loved God with all his heart. He wanted to know as much as possible about God. Josiah studied God's Word and tried his best to obey God every day. During his thirty-one years as king of Judah, he stopped the worship of made-up gods in his kingdom. Josiah told his people about the one true God. Josiah might have been small, but God used him in a *big way!*

What can we learn from Josiah?

Kids can make a big difference in the world for God's kingdom. Josiah was a good king because he wanted to obey God with all his heart. He wasn't afraid to tell the people in his kingdom about God. No matter how little or big we are, God wants us to tell other people about him.

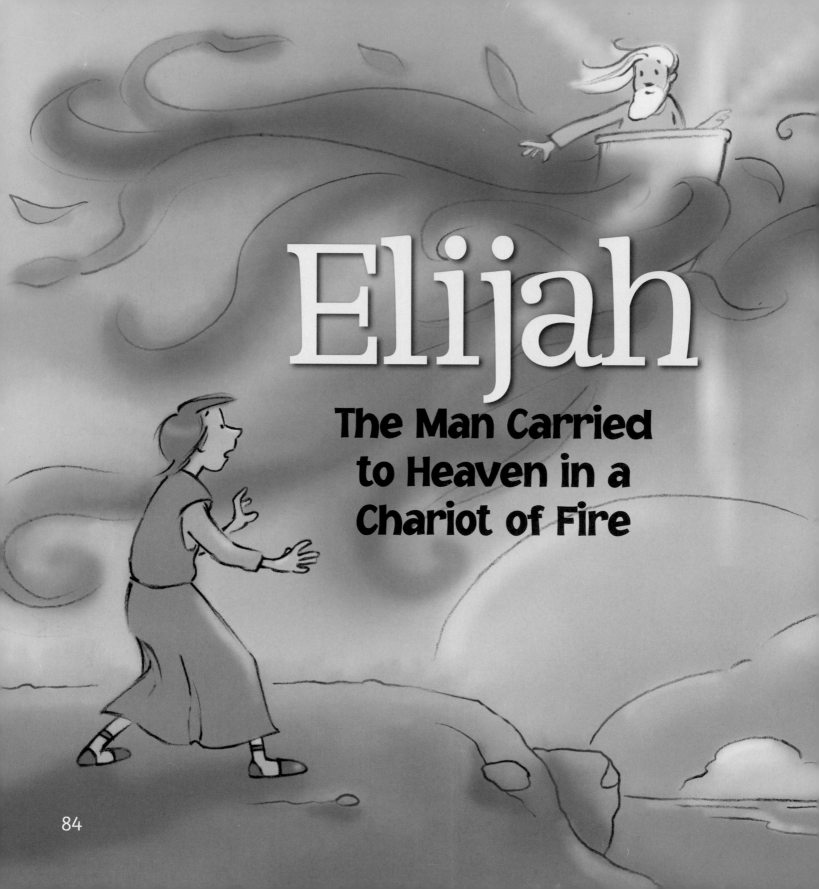

Elijah

The Man Carried to Heaven in a Chariot of Fire

What can we learn from Elijah?

Elijah was a friend to Elisha. Elisha wanted what Elijah had. This is one of the best things about following God. When people see God work in our lives, it can show how great God is!

Elijah was a faithful prophet of God. God showed his power through Elijah. When Elijah prayed for rain, it rained! When he asked God to give food to a widow and her son, God gave them all they needed. When Elijah prayed for God to send fire, God did it! Elijah had a friend named Elisha. Elisha wanted God's power in his life too. Elisha saw God's amazing power when God took Elijah straight to heaven in a chariot of fire and a strong wind! Then Elisha took Elijah's place as a prophet of God.

Elisha

The Man Who Raised a Boy from the Dead

After Elisha saw his friend Elijah carried to heaven in a chariot of fire, he became God's prophet. Elisha gave people messages from God and showed them God's power. One day, Elisha met a woman who was kind to him. She would let Elisha stay at her house as a guest. She and her husband were unable to have children. Elisha told the woman she would have a baby boy, and she did! A few years later, the boy got sick and died. The woman hurried to find Elisha. Elisha prayed and stretched out over the boy's body. The boy sneezed seven times and lived! God showed his power through Elisha.

What can we learn from Elisha?

Elisha learned all about God as he watched Elijah. Because he believed in God's power, he helped to bring a boy back to life. Elisha knew that God can do anything. We can learn about God from watching people who love him. And, like Elisha, we can pray for people who need God's help.

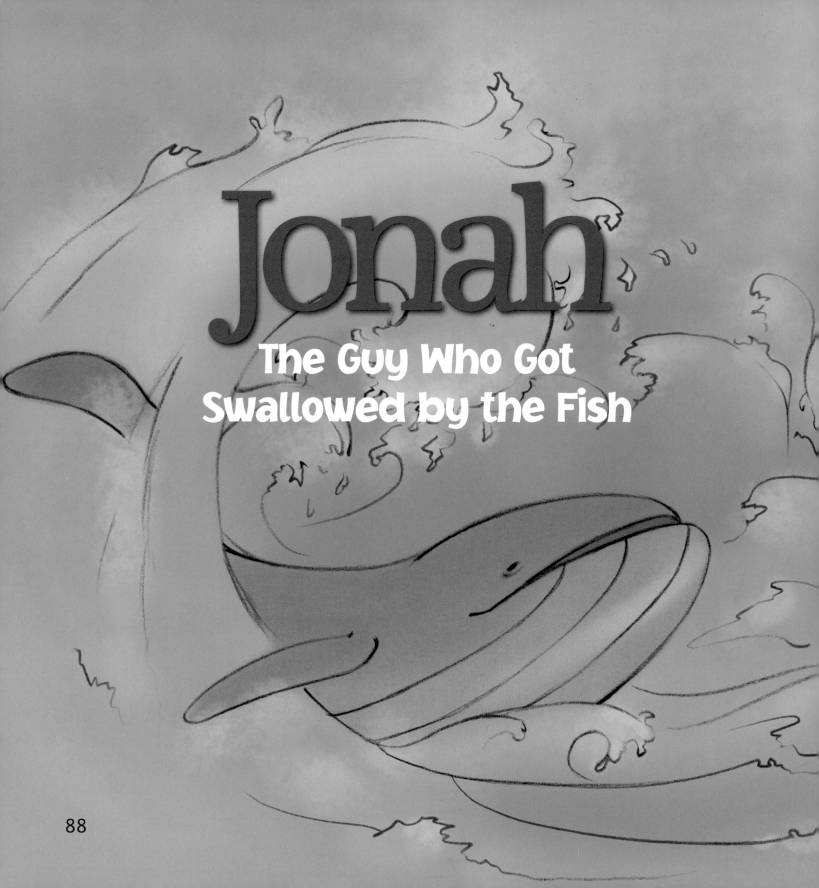

Jonah

The Guy Who Got Swallowed by the Fish

Nineveh was a city where enemies of God's people lived. God told Jonah to travel to Nineveh to warn the people there to stop doing bad things. But Jonah tried to run away on a boat instead of obeying God. He ended up being thrown overboard and swallowed by a big fish. For three days and nights, he prayed inside the fish. God heard him and caused the fish to throw Jonah up onto the land. Jonah finally went to Nineveh and gave the people God's message. The people believed God, and God gave them a second chance. But Jonah wasn't happy about it.

What can we learn from Jonah?

Sometimes it is hard for us to show kindness to mean people. But it's not hard for God to show kindness. We should want to be more like God and be willing to love others—even people who aren't kind to us. We should give people second chances.

The Man Who Loved a Wicked Woman

Hosea was a great man of God. So he must have been surprised when God told him to find a wicked woman to marry. But Hosea obeyed. His wife broke her promise to him time and time again. She left Hosea for another man, and she was sold into slavery. Hosea bought her back. He loved her and forgave her for leaving him.

What can we learn from Hosea?

Hosea's love for his wife helps us to understand God's love for us. We make mistakes. We sin. We run from him. He comes back for us. He even sent his Son Jesus to pay the price for us and set us free from sin. He loves us and forgives us.

Isaiah

The Man Who Saw Things to Come

od spoke to Isaiah through visions, which are like dreams. God gave Isaiah messages to tell the people of Israel. In one vision, God asked Isaiah, "Is there anyone I can send?" God wanted someone to warn his people about the result of their sin. He also wanted his people to know about a Savior—Jesus—who would come to give them hope and forgiveness. Isaiah answered, "I'll go. Send me!" And he did! Isaiah told the people of Israel that Immanuel was coming. *Immanuel* means "God with us."

What can we learn from Isaiah?

Isaiah was willing to do whatever God wanted him to do. Because Isaiah obeyed God, his people had hope. Sometimes God does not need us to do huge things for him. We can love, serve, and obey God right where we are.

The Assyrians

The People Who Worshiped Other Gods

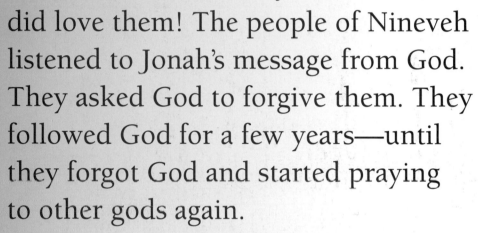

o you remember a man named Jonah? God told Jonah to go to Nineveh. He wanted Jonah to warn the people to stop praying to other gods and treating people badly. Nineveh was the capital of Assyria. Jonah did not think God should love the Assyrians. But God did love them! The people of Nineveh listened to Jonah's message from God. They asked God to forgive them. They followed God for a few years—until they forgot God and started praying to other gods again.

What can we learn from the Assyrians?

Even though the Assyrians prayed to made-up gods and hurt other people, God still loved them! He still wanted them to be his friends! God wants us to be his friends too. No matter what we have done, it is never too late to turn to God!

95

Jeremiah
The Priest and Prophet

Jeremiah was a priest. He was also a prophet. Before Jeremiah was even born, God chose him to give messages to the people of Judah. Jeremiah was supposed to tell them about things that were going to happen to them. God's people were disobeying God and praying to idols. God wanted Jeremiah to speak to them about the effects of their sin. Jeremiah was very young, and he was afraid to speak to so many people! God touched Jeremiah's mouth and gave him the words to say.

What can we learn from Jeremiah?

Jeremiah was scared to do what God asked. After all, he was a young guy! But Jeremiah didn't have anything to worry about because God gave him the words to say. When God asks us to say something, we don't need to be afraid. He will always give us the words.

The Babylonians

The Babylonians were the people from the powerful nation of Babylonia. They were very good at making new things like beautiful art and great cities. They were even known for planting beautiful gardens! The leaders of this great nation decided to attack people in other countries. They wanted to attack God's people living in Judah. God allowed the Babylonians to attack them because the people of Judah needed to be punished for turning away from him.

Great Builders of the Past

What can we learn from the Babylonians?

Just because people may be rich or successful doesn't mean that God is happy with what they are doing. God cares more about our hearts than about the great things we might do.

Ezra

The Man Who Reminded

God had brought the Israelites through so many things. But they had a hard time obeying him. After many years as slaves in another land, they returned to their homeland. When Ezra returned to Jerusalem, he saw that the people had rebuilt God's temple, but they kept making bad choices. Ezra reminded them of who God is. He helped them change their wrong behavior.

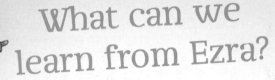

What can we learn from Ezra?

Sometimes our good friends make bad choices. It can be hard not to sin when the people around us are sinning. True friends will speak up and tell their friends when they are doing something wrong. Ezra was a true friend. He saw that his people were not obeying God, and he did something about it!

Nehemiah was a cupbearer to a king. His job was to taste the king's drink before serving it to the king—to make sure no one had poisoned it. Yikes! The king liked Nehemiah and trusted him. One day, Nehemiah bravely asked the king if he could go back to his home. He wanted to help rebuild the wall around the city of Jerusalem. His people were not safe without a wall. The king agreed to let Nehemiah go. He made sure that Nehemiah would be safe and would have all the wood he needed. When Nehemiah and his helpers started building the wall, Jerusalem's neighbors were mad! A wall would protect the people of Jerusalem and make their city strong! People tried to stop them. But God helped Nehemiah and the people keep on building until the wall was finished.

What can we learn from Nehemiah?

It's possible to stop a good idea. But it is not possible to stop God's ideas. Nothing can stop God's good plan for our lives. Nothing can keep us from God's love!

Nehemiah

The Man Who Built a Wall

Esther

The Girl Who Saved Her People

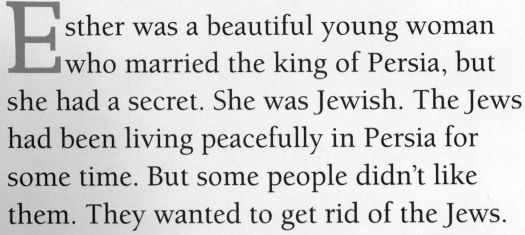

Esther was a beautiful young woman who married the king of Persia, but she had a secret. She was Jewish. The Jews had been living peacefully in Persia for some time. But some people didn't like them. They wanted to get rid of the Jews. Esther found out about an evil plan to hurt her people. She didn't know if she should tell her secret. Esther decided to save her people instead of keeping her secret. Her husband decided to save her people too!

What can we learn from Esther?

Sometimes someone may ask you to keep a secret that should not stay secret. If you are not sure what you should do, ask a parent or another adult.

Mordecai

The Queen's Cousin

Esther's parents died when she was young, so her cousin Mordecai took care of her. After Esther became queen, Mordecai worked in the king's palace. He found out that an evil man named Haman wanted to kill all the Jews in the land. He told Esther to ask the king for help. Esther was afraid to talk to her husband about the Jews—she had never told her husband she was Jewish! She didn't know what would happen to her or to her people if the king found out the truth. But Mordecai said, "It could be that you were made queen for a time like this!" Mordecai's words helped Esther to be brave.

What can we learn from Mordecai?

Esther was a good woman, but she needed help. Mordecai helped Esther do the right thing. God wants us to help our friends follow him and make good choices.

Haman

The King's Mean Official

Haman was one of the worst villains of all time. He was the king's most important helper. Everyone in the kingdom had to bow down to him. Mordecai was a Jew who only would bow to God. He would not kneel down to Haman. This made Haman very mad! He made secret plans to kill Mordecai and get rid of all the Jews. But his plans were not God's plans. When Mordecai found out about Haman's plans, he told Esther. When Esther told the king that Haman was trying to kill her people, the king helped save them from harm.

What can we learn from Haman?

Haman wanted to hurt Mordecai because he didn't like him. God wants us to be kind to our enemies, not hurt them. He wants us to pray for them, not harm them.

Ezekiel

The Prophet Who Saw Dry Bones Live

Ezekiel was God's prophet. God asked him to do some strange things. Ezekiel lay on his left side for more than a year! He burned some of his hair. He dug a tunnel through a wall. He drew a map. He did everything God asked him to do, so the people would know what would happen if they did not obey God. Then God gave Ezekiel a message of hope. Ezekiel saw dry human bones come to life and turn into a whole army of people! This showed Ezekiel that God would never stop loving his people.

What can we learn from Ezekiel?

Ezekiel did a lot of weird things. But he did them because God asked him to do them. Sometimes God asks us to do things that might seem weird to people who don't follow Jesus, like going to church, reading our Bibles, and forgiving people who are unkind to us. All that matters is what God thinks of us!

Daniel
The Guy in the Lions' Den

King Darius really liked Daniel. He placed Daniel in charge of his whole kingdom. This made the other leaders jealous. They talked the king into making a new law that forced everyone to pray only to the king for thirty days. They knew Daniel loved God and would never pray to Darius. Daniel continued to pray to God. He was punished and put into a lions' den. But God sent an angel to protect Daniel from the lions! The king knew God saved Daniel. He told everyone in his kingdom to pray only to God.

What can we learn from Daniel?

Daniel looked like a tasty meal to hungry lions. Still, *nothing* could stop God from saving Daniel. Daniel did not turn away from God, and God did not turn away from Daniel. God will never leave us either!

Shadrach, Meshach,
The Three Friends and a Furnace

King Nebuchadnezzar made a big golden statue and ordered everyone to bow down to it. Shadrach, Meshach, and Abednego only worshiped the one true God. They wouldn't do what the king said, so the king had them thrown into a furnace full of fire. But when the king looked into the furnace, he saw four men walking around—one looked like an angel! The king knew that God had saved Shadrach, Meshach, and Abednego. When they came out of the furnace, they weren't burned at all. They didn't even smell like smoke. King Nebuchadnezzar started believing in God!

and Abednego

What can we learn from Shadrach, Meshach, and Abednego?

These three guys had *big* problems. But they never stopped trusting God, even when it seemed as if they were about to lose their lives. If God can save three men from a blazing fire, just imagine what he can do when we face problems.

King Nebuchadnezzar

The King Who Went Crazy

King Nebuchadnezzar had a real whopper of a weird dream, but he couldn't figure out what the dream meant. Daniel told the king the meaning of his dream. Because Nebuchadnezzar was proud and didn't think God was in charge, God would punish him for seven years. He would live out in the wild and eat grass like an animal. His hair and fingernails would grow long. The dream came true. Seven years later, Nebuchadnezzar prayed to God, and God allowed him to rule his kingdom again.

What can we learn from King Nebuchadnezzar?

King Nebuchadnezzar thought he didn't need God. God showed him the truth. Sometimes God teaches us his truth in ways we don't like. But he wants us to learn that he is in charge and that he loves us.

Mary

The Mother
of Jesus

Mary was a young girl who loved God. One day, an angel named Gabriel talked to Mary. He told her that God had chosen her to have a baby boy. This boy would be the Son of God! But Mary was confused. She was not married yet. The angel told her that nothing is impossible for God. She would have the baby and name him Jesus.

What can we learn from Mary? ⭐

God chose Mary to be Jesus' mother. She was just a girl like other girls. Yet she loved a great God. Mary is living proof that God uses normal, everyday people to do big things.

Zechariah

The Father of John the Baptist

Zechariah was a priest who loved and obeyed God. He and his wife, Elizabeth, had no children. One day, Zechariah was chosen for a special job. Some priests waited their entire lives for this job. He would burn incense in the temple. Burnt incense makes a sweet-smelling smoke. God's people believed the smoke would carry their prayers up to God! As Zechariah burned the incense, an angel named Gabriel appeared and told Zechariah that God had heard his prayers. He and Elizabeth would have a boy named John! Zechariah was old, and he didn't believe it could be possible for him to have a son. Because Zechariah doubted God, the angel made him unable to talk until John was born.

What can we learn from Zechariah?

God waited until the right time to answer Zechariah's prayers for a child. God always hears our prayers. He listens to us and answers us in his perfect time.

Elizabeth

The Mother of John the Baptist

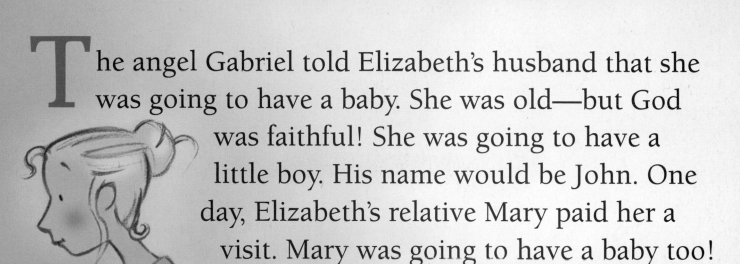

The angel Gabriel told Elizabeth's husband that she was going to have a baby. She was old—but God was faithful! She was going to have a little boy. His name would be John. One day, Elizabeth's relative Mary paid her a visit. Mary was going to have a baby too! That baby was Jesus. Elizabeth felt her baby jump for joy inside her when she heard Mary's voice. Elizabeth believed Mary's baby was the Son of God!

What can we learn from Elizabeth?

Elizabeth is one of the faithful women we learn about in the Bible. God gave her the gift of a baby, even when it seemed impossible. She believed God and knew God had answered her prayers. Her life shows us God's power.

Joseph

The Husband of Mary

Joseph was going to be married to Mary when he found out she was pregnant. Joseph didn't understand what was happening. He decided to call off the wedding. But an angel told Joseph the Holy Spirit had placed the baby inside Mary. The angel also told Joseph to name the baby Jesus. Joseph did what the angel said. He and Mary were soon married, and Joseph helped raise Jesus, the Son of God.

What can we learn from Joseph?

Joseph was confused, but he chose to trust what God had to say to him through the angel. We should always listen to God and believe him, even when things don't make sense to us.

Simeon

The Old Man Who Held Jesus

Mary and Joseph obeyed Jewish rules. Those rules said new babies had to be brought to the temple. So, they brought baby Jesus. They also had to bring a special present to God—either two doves or two pigeons. But when they walked into the temple, something strange happened. An old man swept Jesus up in his arms. The man's name was Simeon. God had promised Simeon that he would see Jesus before he died. Simeon had been waiting for this day to come. He joyfully praised God! Simeon told Mary that Jesus would be very special.

What can we learn from Simeon?

When Mary and Joseph brought Jesus into the temple, Simeon knew right away that the baby was his Lord and Savior. Like Simeon, we can trust in God's promises. Jesus is coming again someday. We can joyfully look forward to that day when we will see him face to face.

127

James

The Brother of Jesus

James and Jesus were brothers. Their mom was Mary. Jesus was the Son of God. James was the son of Joseph, who was a carpenter. We don't know much about Jesus and James' childhood, but maybe they spent their days playing in Joseph's workshop. James didn't grow up believing Jesus was the Son of God. He thought Jesus was just showing off. But after Jesus died and rose again, he appeared to James, and James finally believed! His brother had been the Son of God all along. James told the truth about Jesus to many people and became a leader of the church in Jerusalem.

What can we learn from Jesus' brother James?

James did not accept his brother. Sometimes we might feel that people in our families don't accept us. It can make us feel alone. Jesus understands. We are never alone!

John the Baptist

The Man Who Baptized Jesus

John was a miracle baby. His parents were both very old when he was born. The angel Gabriel told John's dad, Zechariah, that John would have a special job. He would tell people about Jesus, the Son of God. When John grew up, he talked about Jesus to everyone. He baptized people who wanted their sins forgiven. Jesus himself asked John to baptize him. John was shocked! Jesus never sinned and certainly didn't need forgiveness. John said to Jesus, "I should be baptized by you." But Jesus insisted. He wanted to set a good example for all people. John had the important job of baptizing Jesus, the Savior of the world.

What can we learn from John the Baptist?

John couldn't believe that he got to baptize Jesus, the Son of God. It's important for us to remember that Jesus loves us and made us for important jobs too. God made you for a special reason!

Andrew

The Man Who Witnessed a Miracle

Andrew was a fisherman. He was also Simon Peter's brother. When Jesus called both men to follow him, they dropped their fishing nets and followed him right away. They would be fishers of people instead of fish. Andrew was with Jesus when he spoke to a crowd of more than 5,000 hungry people. Andrew found a boy with five loaves of bread and two fish. He watched in wonder as Jesus fed the crowd with that one small meal.

What can we learn from Andrew?

Andrew knew what was important in life. He was willing to leave his job behind to follow Jesus. He had the honor of traveling with Jesus and seeing powerful miracles. Nothing should be more important in our lives than following Jesus.

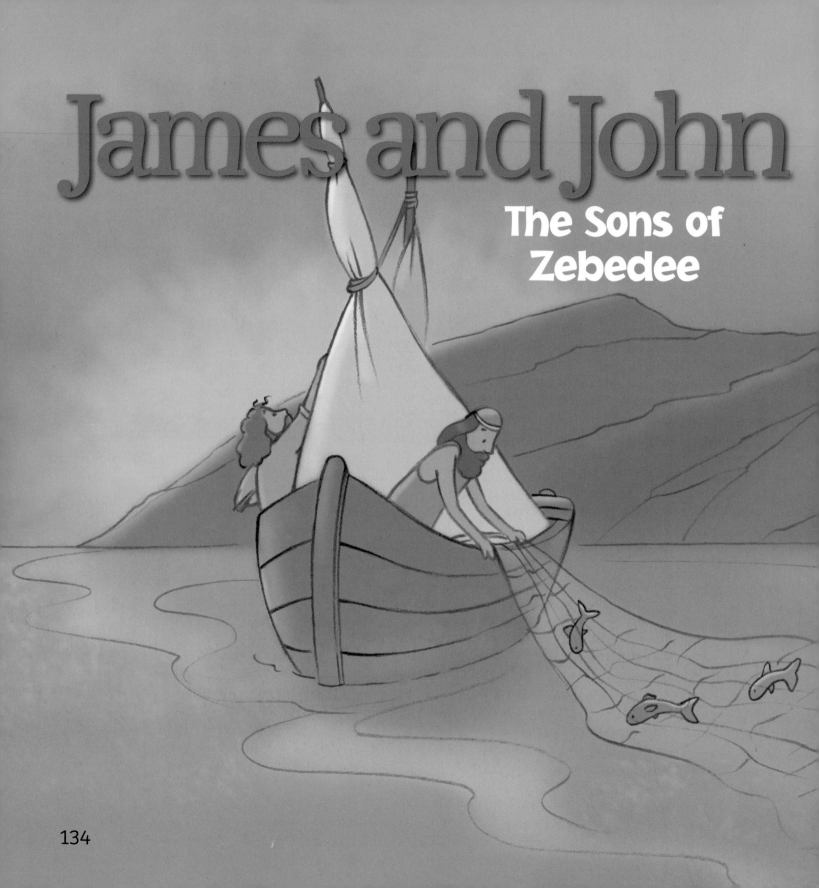

James and John

The Sons of
Zebedee

James and John were brothers. They worked as fishermen with their dad, Zebedee. The brothers quickly left their boat and their dad when Jesus asked them to follow him. Jesus gave them the nickname "thunderbolts." They didn't always think before they spoke, and Jesus had to explain their mistakes to them more than once. But they were still Jesus' special friends. They were chosen to go with Jesus up a mountain to talk with Moses and Elijah. James and John saw Jesus raise a girl from the dead!

What can we learn from James and John?

James and John left their jobs and their family so they could follow Jesus. They didn't always say or do everything perfectly, but Jesus never stopped being their friend. When we make mistakes, we can remember that Jesus will not stop being our friend. We can learn from our mistakes and become better followers of Jesus.

135

Matthew

The Tax Collector

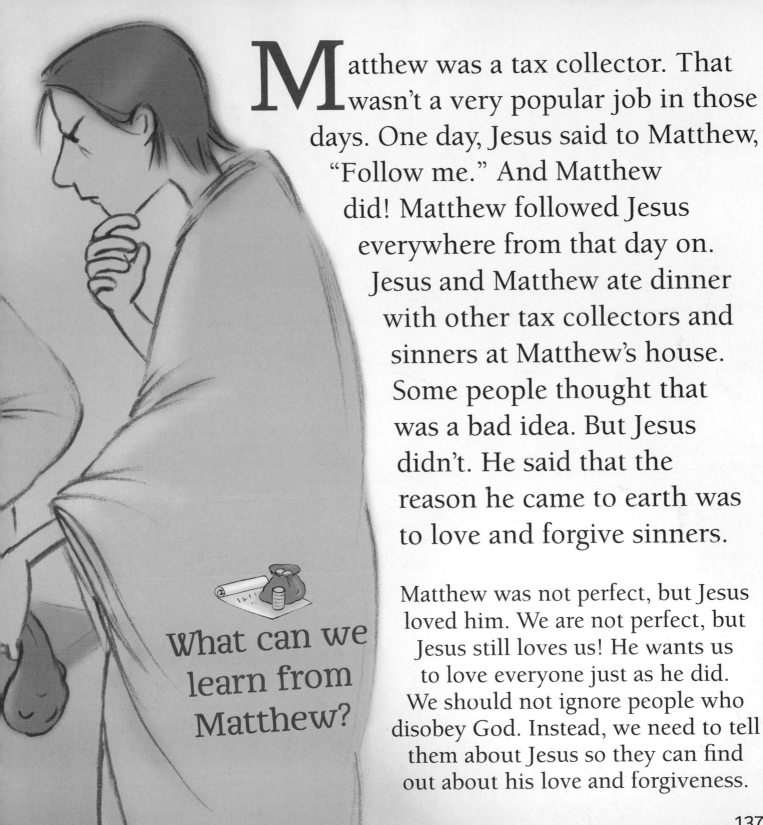

M atthew was a tax collector. That wasn't a very popular job in those days. One day, Jesus said to Matthew, "Follow me." And Matthew did! Matthew followed Jesus everywhere from that day on. Jesus and Matthew ate dinner with other tax collectors and sinners at Matthew's house. Some people thought that was a bad idea. But Jesus didn't. He said that the reason he came to earth was to love and forgive sinners.

What can we learn from Matthew?

Matthew was not perfect, but Jesus loved him. We are not perfect, but Jesus still loves us! He wants us to love everyone just as he did. We should not ignore people who disobey God. Instead, we need to tell them about Jesus so they can find out about his love and forgiveness.

Simon Peter

The Man Who Walked on Water

What can we learn from Simon Peter?

Sometimes life can be scary. But if we keep our eyes on Jesus, he will keep us safe. If Jesus tells us we can do something, he will help us do it. We can trust him!

Jesus went up a mountain to pray while his disciples were on a boat. A big storm came in the middle of the night, and the disciples were far from the shore. Jesus walked on top of the water to reach the boat. Peter was scared at first, but he was also amazed. He said, "Lord, if it is really you, tell me to come to you on the water." Jesus said, "Come on!" Peter walked on water! But then Peter remembered the storm, and he began to sink. Jesus reached out his hand and saved him. "Why do you doubt?" Jesus asked.

The Samaritan

The Woman at the Well

Woman

In the days of Jesus, Jews and Samaritans didn't get along very well. Some Jews believed that Samaritans were dirty. Yet Jesus stopped at a Samaritan well. A woman was getting water. Jesus asked her for a drink. As they talked, Jesus offered her a kind of water she couldn't drink. He wanted to give her living water, which is his gift of eternal life.

What can we learn from the Samaritan woman?

We sometimes look at people and decide if they are good or bad. Jesus saw everyone the same. He loves everyone no matter what their skin color is or where they live. No one is better than anyone else. We should love everyone as Jesus did.

The Rich Young Man

The Eye-of-the-Needle Man

One day, a rich young man came to talk to Jesus. He wanted to know how to live forever in heaven. Jesus told him to follow the Ten Commandments. But the man already did. So Jesus told him to sell everything he owned and give it to the poor. *Everything?* The man did not like that. Jesus said it is very hard for a rich man to enter heaven. It is easier for a camel to go through the eye of a tiny needle. Yet all things are possible with God.

What can we learn from the rich young man?

Because of Jesus, we can have eternal life. We only have to believe that Jesus is the Son of God and that he died to take the punishment for our sins. But God still wants us to be good people and love others.

The Sick Woman Healed in the Crowd

The Woman Who Was Healed by Touching Jesus' Clothes

Everywhere Jesus went, people wanted to see him. The crowds were so large. The people pushed and shoved. One woman was very sick. She reached out as far as she could. She only wanted to touch the bottom edge of Jesus' clothes. The moment her fingers finally touched Jesus, she was healed of her sickness! Jesus asked, "Who touched me?" He felt her touch in the middle of the crowd. The woman's faith was so big!

What can we learn from the sick woman?

This woman was sick. She wanted to be healthy. She knew Jesus could help her. He felt her touch. When we reach out for Jesus, he always notices us too.

145

The Blind Man

The Man Who Was Healed with Mud

Jesus and his disciples passed by a man who had been blind since birth. The blind man didn't ask to be healed. He couldn't see Jesus. But Jesus had a heart for people in need. Jesus could have chosen any way to heal the blind man, but the way he healed him was a surprise. Jesus spit on the ground and made some mud. Then he wiped the mud in the man's eyes. After the man washed the mud off his eyes in a pool, he could see!

What can we learn from the blind man?

The blind man couldn't see Jesus. But Jesus saw him. Sometimes we may feel as if Jesus isn't with us because we can't see him. But we do not need to worry. He always sees us! He is with us, and he will help us when we need it.

Zacchaeus

The Guy Who Climbed the Tree to See Jesus

A large crowd had gathered to see Jesus. One man who wanted to see him was too short. He couldn't see over the heads and shoulders of others in the crowd. His name was Zacchaeus. He climbed a tree so he could get a better view. Zacchaeus got to see Jesus, and Jesus saw him too. Jesus walked over to Zacchaeus and asked him to come down. Jesus was going to Zacchaeus's house!

What can we learn from Zacchaeus?

Zacchaeus wanted to see Jesus. He didn't stop until he found a way— up a tree. He wanted to get as close to Jesus as he could. Jesus saw him and got closer to *him*. Jesus will always meet us when we want to be close to him and spend time with him.

149

The Paralyzed Man

The Man Lowered through a Roof

Jesus was teaching at the home of a friend when something really strange happened. A man was paralyzed. He couldn't walk. His friends knew Jesus could help, but they couldn't get in the house because it was too crowded with people. So his friends made a way. They lowered him through a hole in the roof. First, Jesus told the paralyzed man, "Your sins are forgiven." Then Jesus said, "Get up! Pick up your mat and walk home." And he did! Because of the man's faith, Jesus healed him.

What can we learn from the paralyzed man?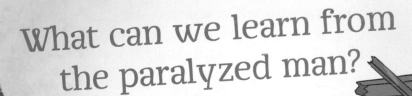

The paralyzed man and his friends didn't give up trying to reach Jesus. Because of their great faith, Jesus helped them. When times get tough in our lives, we can always rely on Jesus. He will reward our faith.

Gave Everything

The Poor Woman Who Gave Her Last Coins

One day, Jesus watched people bring their gifts of money to the temple. Rich people gave large amounts of money. Then Jesus spotted a poor widow. She had only two small coins. She gave those two coins to the temple for God's use. Jesus said that her gift was so much bigger than anyone else's gift. The rich people would still have many riches to go home to. The widow had given all she had to give.

What can we learn from the widow who gave everything?

The widow gave God her very best.
She couldn't have given any more.
The rich people gave from their pockets.
The woman gave from her heart.

The Lost Son

The Son Who Returned to His Father

A father had two sons. The younger son wanted to leave home. He asked his father for his share of the family's money. So the father gave the money to his son, and the son left home. He went to another country and wasted all the money. He had nothing left, and he became hungry. He wanted to go back home, but he thought his father would be angry when he saw him. Instead, his father ran to him, hugged him, and cooked him a feast fit for a king!

What can we learn from the lost son?

Sometimes people run from God and are afraid to come home. But God is a good and loving Father. Jesus died on the cross to take away God's anger. He will always welcome us, no matter what we have done!

Mary and Martha

The Two Sisters

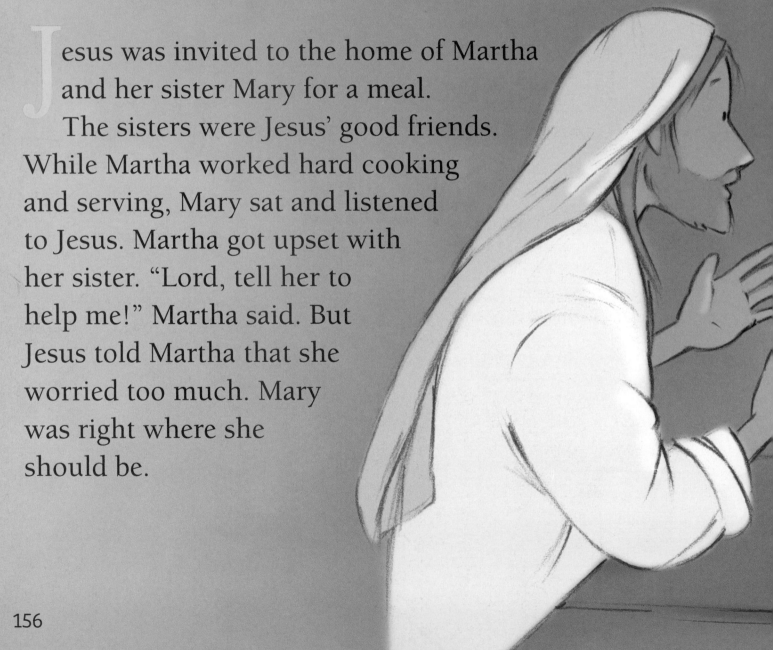

Jesus was invited to the home of Martha and her sister Mary for a meal. The sisters were Jesus' good friends. While Martha worked hard cooking and serving, Mary sat and listened to Jesus. Martha got upset with her sister. "Lord, tell her to help me!" Martha said. But Jesus told Martha that she worried too much. Mary was right where she should be.

What can we learn from Mary and Martha?

It is good to serve others and to do good things. It is good to be busy for the Lord. But we should never be too busy to spend time with God.

Lazarus

The Dead Man Who Lived

Lazarus was Mary and Martha's brother. He was also Jesus' good friend. Lazarus had become very sick. The sisters called for Jesus to come help, but he didn't show up right away. By the time Jesus showed up, Lazarus was already dead and his body was starting to smell! Martha and Mary were upset. Jesus was too late! Jesus cried. He prayed out loud and asked God to let the people believe he was God's Son. Then he shouted, "Lazarus, come out!" And he did. Lazarus lived!

What can we learn from Lazarus?

Lazarus's family thought that Jesus was too late. But Jesus is never too late. Nothing is too hard for him. He is always right on time! When things go wrong in our lives, Jesus will always show up, even if it is not in the way we had planned.

Scribes and Pharisees

The Unloving Religious Leaders

The Pharisees and scribes were the leaders of the Jewish people. They carefully read the Old Testament. They read the words of Moses, who said the Messiah—Jesus—would come to save us all. Still, many of them did not believe Jesus, the Son of God, when he came and spoke to them and did miracles. When Jesus healed someone on the Sabbath, the Pharisees and scribes were angry. Their man-made rules didn't allow people to work on the Sabbath. They loved their rules more than they loved people.

What can we learn from the scribes and Pharisees?

Loving people is one of the best things we can do. It's more important than anything else. We should always do what's right, even if it's not what others do.

Caiaphas

The Man Who Condemned Jesus

It was written long ago that the Messiah (or King) would come. Jesus was the Messiah. The news about Jesus and his miracles had spread quickly. More and more people were following his teachings. Caiaphas was the Jewish high priest. He did not accept Jesus or believe in him. He had a mean plan to get rid of Jesus so the people wouldn't follow him. Caiaphas sent Jesus to a Roman leader to be punished by death on the cross.

What can we learn from Caiaphas?

Caiaphas was a selfish person. He only thought about himself. He did not want to follow God's plan. Rather than be selfish like Caiaphas, ask God to help you follow and serve Jesus.

Judas Iscariot

The Disciple Who Betrayed Jesus

Judas was Jesus' friend. For three years they traveled, ate, and lived together. Even though Jesus had been a friend to him, Judas was not loyal to Jesus. Judas helped the chief priests arrest Jesus, and they paid him thirty silver coins. The chief priests did not like Jesus. They planned a way to kill him. They sent a large crowd of men with swords and clubs to arrest Jesus. Judas went with them. He kissed Jesus to show the men who Jesus was. The men grabbed Jesus and arrested him.

What can we learn from Judas Iscariot?

God is not surprised when people turn away from him. God can use a person's bad choices to accomplish his plan for the world.

Pontius Pilate

The Man Who Didn't Stand Up for Jesus

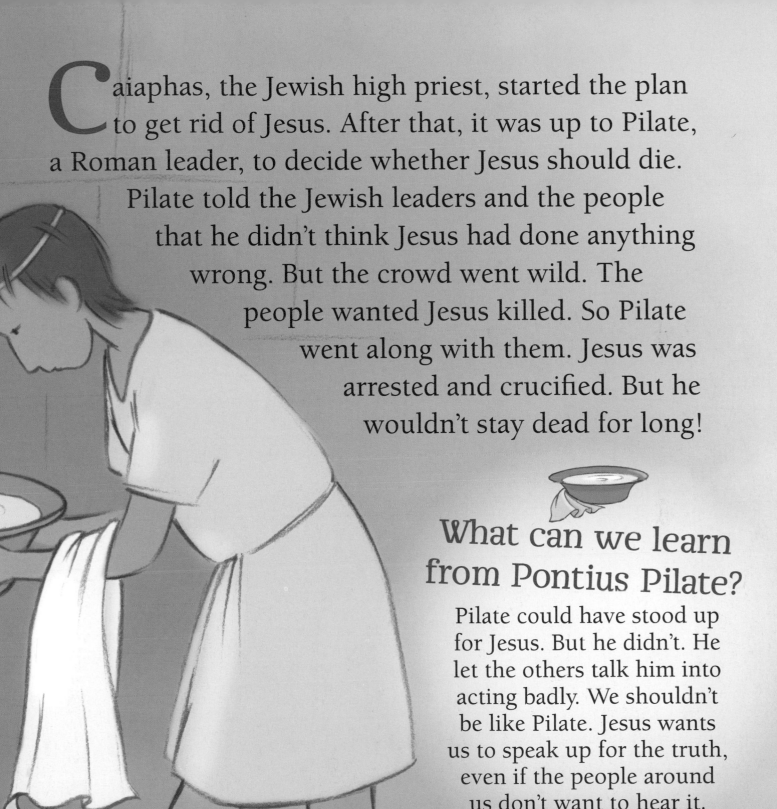

Caiaphas, the Jewish high priest, started the plan to get rid of Jesus. After that, it was up to Pilate, a Roman leader, to decide whether Jesus should die. Pilate told the Jewish leaders and the people that he didn't think Jesus had done anything wrong. But the crowd went wild. The people wanted Jesus killed. So Pilate went along with them. Jesus was arrested and crucified. But he wouldn't stay dead for long!

What can we learn from Pontius Pilate?

Pilate could have stood up for Jesus. But he didn't. He let the others talk him into acting badly. We shouldn't be like Pilate. Jesus wants us to speak up for the truth, even if the people around us don't want to hear it.

Jesus The Son of God

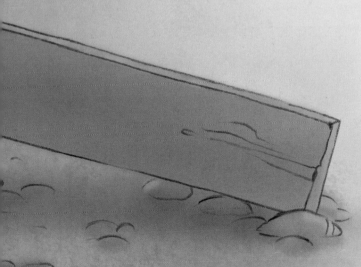

Jesus, the Son of God and King of kings, came to earth in a most surprising way. He didn't show up with a crown or rule from a mighty throne. He was born as a human baby, and he was put in a manger full of hay. Jesus treated people with grace, mercy, and love. He did great miracles and taught people how to love and forgive. He gave his own life in our place when he died on the cross. He beat Satan. He rose again! He did all this so that we might be saved from our sin and live as children of God.

What can we learn from Jesus?

Jesus was born as a helpless baby, yet he is the Son of God. He was a normal boy and powerful God at the same time. This is what made him so different. Jesus was the perfect example of what it means to be God's child. Because of Jesus, we can be children of God too!

Mary Magdalene

The Devoted Friend of Jesus

Mary Magdalene became a follower of Jesus after he saved her from seven evil spirits that were controlling her. She and a few other women traveled with Jesus and his disciples throughout Galilee. The women gave what they had to take care of Jesus and the disciples. Mary Magdalene was there at the cross when Jesus died. She was also the first person to see Jesus after he rose from the dead!

What can we learn from Mary Magdalene?

Mary Magdalene was healed and forgiven by Jesus. She became a new woman! Jesus changes hearts. There is no one who is too bad for Jesus to love or to help!

Nicodemus

The Pharisee Who Trusted Jesus

Most Pharisees didn't like Jesus very much. But Nicodemus was different. He went to Jesus one night, and Jesus told him that God loved everyone. He also told Nicodemus that God had sent his only Son as a gift. Everyone who believes in Jesus will get to live with God forever. Nicodemus believed Jesus was God's Son. After Jesus died, Nicodemus helped prepare his body to be buried.

What can we learn from Nicodemus?

Nicodemus was brave. He didn't follow his friends. He believed in Jesus. Our family and friends may not believe in Jesus, but we can still do the right thing and trust him.

Thomas
The Doubting Disciple

After Jesus rose again, the disciples saw him with their own eyes! But Thomas wasn't in the room with them when Jesus showed up that day. Thomas wasn't sure if Jesus was really alive. He said he needed proof. He wouldn't believe it unless he could see and feel the scars on Jesus' hands and side. When Thomas saw Jesus, Jesus said, "Look at my hands! Put your hand in my side, Thomas. Stop doubting." Thomas saw and believed for himself!

174

What can we learn from Thomas?

Jesus said that people who believe in him even when they don't see him with their eyes are truly blessed. That's us! We do not have to doubt. We can believe that Jesus died and rose again and that our sins are forgiven.

Stephen
The First Christian Martyr

After Jesus went back to heaven, more and more people started believing in him. Stephen was one of those people. He was chosen to serve food to poor widows. God gave Stephen power to do miracles and tell people the truth about Jesus. Some men who did not love Jesus told lies about Stephen and had him arrested. The Jewish leaders threw stones at Stephen and killed him! Shortly before he was killed, Stephen looked up and saw Jesus standing at God's right side, welcoming Stephen home to heaven.

What can we learn from Stephen?

When we are scared or sad, Jesus is always with us. He was with Stephen every step of the way. As Stephen died, Jesus was waiting for him!

177

Philip and the Ethiopian Man

The Teacher and the Student

Philip traveled around telling people about Jesus. One day, an angel told Philip to walk along a desert road. So he did. He saw a chariot down the road, and God told him to catch up to it. Philip ran to it and heard a man reading about Jesus from God's Word. The man had come from the faraway land of Ethiopia to pray in the Jewish temple. But he didn't understand what he was reading. Philip climbed into the chariot and explained it to him. The man put his trust in Jesus, and Philip baptized him.

What can we learn from Philip and the Ethiopian man?

The Ethiopian man knew that Jesus was real. He traveled far to honor God. He didn't understand the Bible yet, but God sent Philip to help him. God puts people in the right places at the right times to help others understand the truth about Jesus.

Saul/Paul

The Man Who Changed His Life and His Name

Many people wanted to arrest Jesus' followers, including a man named Saul. He walked along the road to Damascus one day on his way to arrest more believers. A bright light came down that left him blind. Saul heard a voice saying, "Saul! Saul! Why are you so cruel to me?" It was Jesus! When Saul got to Damascus, God sent a man named Ananias to heal Saul of his blindness. From then on, Saul told everyone he met about the truth of Jesus. Saul ended up changing his name to Paul. He was a changed man!

What can we learn from Saul/Paul?

Paul was on his way to arrest Jesus' followers. But it only took hearing Jesus' voice to change Paul's life forever. Jesus can change our lives in the blink of an eye. There is nothing too hard for him. There is no one too bad for him to change.

Barnabas

The Traveling Messenger

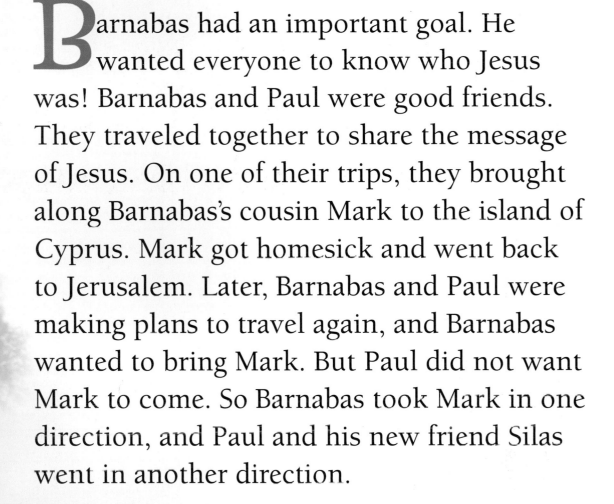

Barnabas had an important goal. He wanted everyone to know who Jesus was! Barnabas and Paul were good friends. They traveled together to share the message of Jesus. On one of their trips, they brought along Barnabas's cousin Mark to the island of Cyprus. Mark got homesick and went back to Jerusalem. Later, Barnabas and Paul were making plans to travel again, and Barnabas wanted to bring Mark. But Paul did not want Mark to come. So Barnabas took Mark in one direction, and Paul and his new friend Silas went in another direction.

What can we learn from Barnabas?

Paul and Barnabas didn't always agree with each other. But they were friends who wanted the same thing—to tell other people about Jesus. We sometimes disagree with our friends. But we can't allow little fights to ruin our friendships or keep us from telling other people about Jesus.

Timothy

The Young Leader

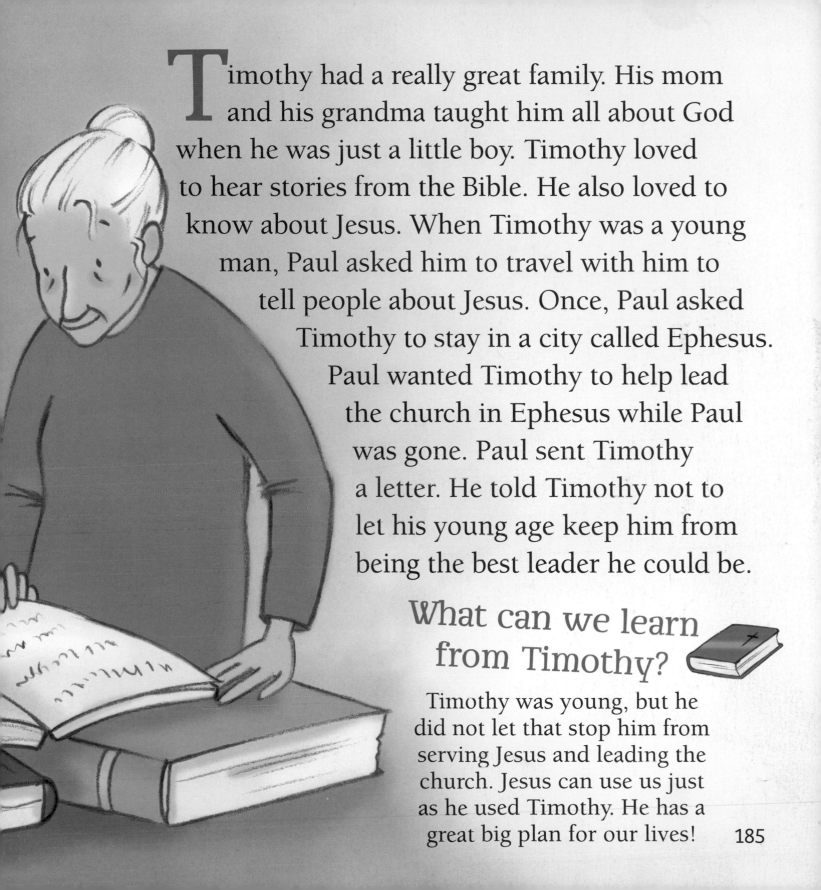

Timothy had a really great family. His mom and his grandma taught him all about God when he was just a little boy. Timothy loved to hear stories from the Bible. He also loved to know about Jesus. When Timothy was a young man, Paul asked him to travel with him to tell people about Jesus. Once, Paul asked Timothy to stay in a city called Ephesus. Paul wanted Timothy to help lead the church in Ephesus while Paul was gone. Paul sent Timothy a letter. He told Timothy not to let his young age keep him from being the best leader he could be.

What can we learn from Timothy?

Timothy was young, but he did not let that stop him from serving Jesus and leading the church. Jesus can use us just as he used Timothy. He has a great big plan for our lives! 185

God

The Bible Is His Story

All the stories of the Bible add up to one big story: God's story. He is the main character! God created this universe and everything in it. He created each and every person in history. He sees and hears everything. He watches out for his children and loves them very much! And best of all, he wants you to know him!

What can we learn from God?

God is good—always. He cannot be unfair. He cannot lie. Sometimes it can be hard for us to imagine this. God wants every person to know him too. That's why he sent Jesus to earth. The better we know and follow Jesus, the more we will understand God!

Index